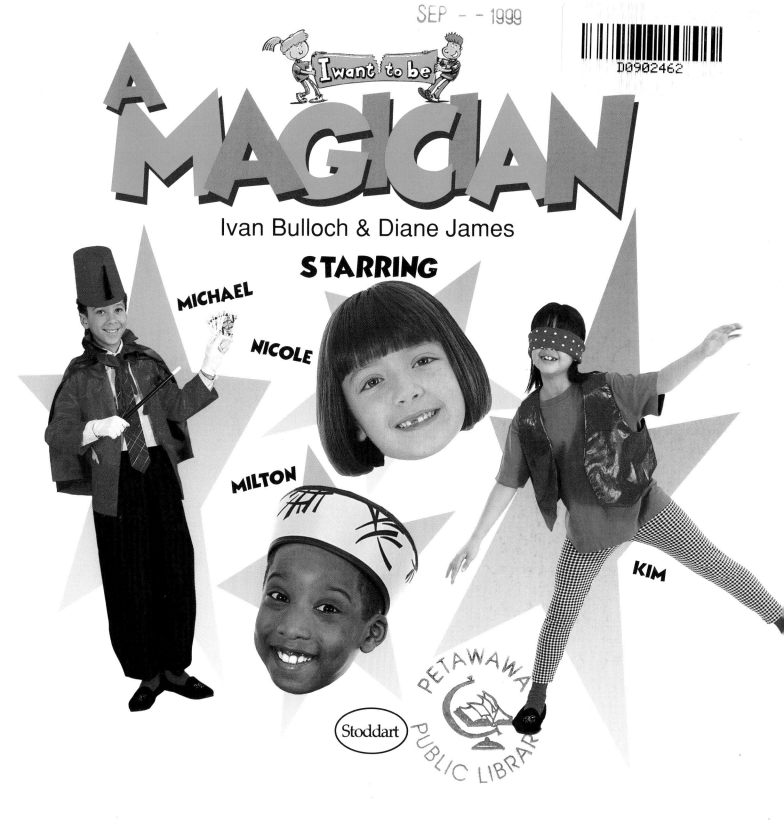

# I want to be
# A MAGICIAN

Ivan Bulloch & Diane James

## STARRING

MICHAEL

NICOLE

MILTON

KIM

Stoddart

**Consultant** Otis Earle
**Photographs** © Fiona Pragoff
**Illustrations** Debi Ani
**Design Assistant** Peter Clayman

Published in Canada in 1995 by
Stoddart Publishing Co. Limited
34 Lesmill Road, Toronto, Canada, M3B 2T6

Printed and bound by G. Canale and C.S.p.A, Italy

**Canadian Cataloguing in Publication Data**

Main entry under title:

I want to be a magician

ISBN 0-7737-5759-7
1. Conjuring — Juvenile literature.  2. Magicians —
Juvenile literature.  I. Pragoff, Fiona.
II. Matthews, Debi Ani.  III. Matthews, Derrek.
IV. Title: A magician.

GV1548.I2 1995          j793.8          C95-931132-7

BUL
J

30p. ill. 22cm

# CONTENTS

# I WANT TO BE A MAGICIAN

As soon as your friends discover your amazing new skills they will want you to perform for them. You'll need to set aside quite a bit of time for practising to perfect your act. Always remember the golden rule which is NEVER tell anyone how a trick is performed. Also, remember that performing the same trick twice in a row is asking for trouble!

Make a special hat to help the magic work!

Even simple props, like a piece of string and a pair of scissors, can be used to make magic!

Making something appear as if from nowhere is one of the best tricks you can do!

All magicians have a few card tricks up their sleeve

Some tricks need to be set up beforehand – just like this secret shelf!

When you have learned enough tricks it will be time to put on a show for your friends. Later in the book you will find some tips to help with the preparations.

# IT'S SO EASY!

**Some tricks are so simple you can perform them anywhere! Good magicians always have plenty of pockets to keep handy props!**

Flick your wrist quickly downwards and the pencil will appear as if by magic!

### Pencil power

This is a really snappy trick and all you need is an elastic band and a pencil. Choose an elastic band that is as close to your skin colour as possible.

### The invisible ball

Hold the edge of a paper bag as though you were going to click your fingers. Ask someone to throw an imaginary ball into the bag. Just as the ball is about to land in the bag, click your fingers and pretend to catch the ball. The noise will sound just like a real ball falling in the bag!

Don't let anyone see this side of your hand!

PLOP!

Attach the pencil to the back of your hand with the elastic band. Don't let the person you are trying this trick out on see the pencil! Tell them you can make a pencil appear out of thin air.

## Double your money

This trick will take a few seconds to set up! Open a magazine and lay three coins on a page. Turn over a couple of pages to cover up the coins. Tell a friend that you can magically double their money.

## Floating pencil

This is an amazingly easy trick, but very effective! Stand sideways to your audience and put a pencil on the palm of one hand. Using the other hand grip hold of your wrist.

Ask them to put three coins on the empty page. Shut the magazine up. Say the magic words and gently shake the magazine. Out will fall six coins.

Turn the hand with the pencil so that the audience only see the back of it. As you turn your hand, secretly place your forefinger on the pencil. This will keep it in position. The audience will think the pencil is floating in mid air!

# PAPER MAGIC

**It's just amazing what you can do with a few pieces of paper! You can make a tree appear in a flash and create two separate rings from one strip of paper.**

**Paper palm**
Take a sheet of newspaper. Roll it up starting from one of the short ends.

Secure the end with a piece of sticky tape.

Use a pair of scissors to make cuts through all the layers. Start at one end of the roll and cut to about half way down. After a bit of practice, you will be able to do all of this easily in a matter of seconds.

Now for the real magic! With a big flourish, gently pull the centre layers upwards. As you pull you will gradually reveal a giant palm tree!

Try coloured wrapping paper instead of newspaper for an extra special tree

## Paper rings

Tell your audience that you can turn a single strip of paper into two interlinked loops. All you need is a pair of scissors and some sticky tape.

Take the strip of paper and make two twists in it. Tape the ends together.

*I surprise myself every time I do this trick!*

Using the scissors, cut the loop you have made down the middle. Keep going all the way round. Now for the magic!

When you pull the loop apart you will have two rings joined together!

# HATS OFF!

**Every magician needs a hat! It will help you feel the part and show your audience that you are a professional!**

Here are some ideas for making your own hats. You'll need thin coloured card for the top hat, and sticky back felt and thin cord for the fez. You'll also need a pair of scissors and glue.

### Top Hat

Decide how tall you want your hat. Cut a rectangle of card to this height.

It should be long enough to fit round your head. Glue the ends together to make a cylinder. Draw round one of the ends of the hat and cut out a circle of card to make the top.

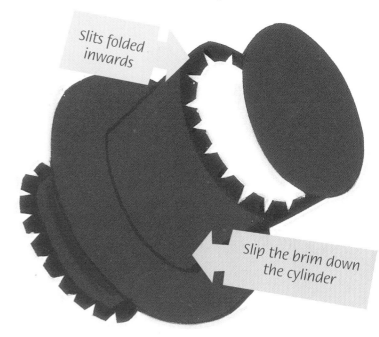

*Slits folded inwards*

*Slip the brim down the cylinder*

For the brim, draw round one of the ends again. Then draw a wider circle around it. Cut round both circles. Now make slits at both ends of the cylinder. Fold the slits at the tops inwards and the bottom ones outwards. Glue the surface of the slits. Stick the top of the hat on and then slip the brim down the cylinder.

*Cut glittery stars from wrapping paper or foil and glue them on*

## Fez

Take a piece of sticky back felt about 60cm long and cut a shape like the one above. Cut a card shape the same size. Stick the two together. Curve the shape around your head. When it fits glue the edges together. Make slits around the top edge and fold them inwards.

To finish off your fez, make a tassel. Wind some thin black cord round and round a rectangle of card. Snip through the cord at one end. Slip the cord off the card carefully. At the uncut end, tie a short length round to secure it.

Don't use too much cord or it will be difficult to cut.

Use a needle and cotton to attach the tassel to the top of your fez.

Glue the circle onto the tabs.

Draw around the top of your hat and cut out a circle from felt and card.

# SECRET STRETCH

**The secret ingredient in both of these tricks is a length of stretchy elastic. It can make a key seem to vanish and a magic wand appear to rise of its own free will!**

Pull the key out with your right thumb and first finger and hold it on the palm of your left hand. Don't ever let your audience see the elastic!

Make sure the safety pin is secure

Keep that elastic well hidden!

### Vanishing key
Tie one end of a length of elastic – about 30cm long – to a key, and the other end to a large safety pin. Attach the safety pin to the top of one of your jacket sleeves. You may need to adjust the length of the elastic to make sure that the key does not show below your sleeve.

Pretend that you are taking the key in your left hand by making a fist. Let the key whizz back out of sight up your sleeve. Now show the audience both hands. Where is the key?

## Magic wand

No matter how many times you push this wand back into your hand, it still insists on rising back up again!

Make a show of 'talking' to the wand. Tell it to stop playing around!

Cut a 25cm length of plastic tubing. You can buy this from a hardware shop. You also need two white buttons with shanks, exactly the same diameter as the tubing, and a 20cm length of elastic. Glue a length of black paper round the wand and add short strips of white paper at either end.

Take one of the buttons between your thumb and first finger and pull the button and elastic out and up along the side of the wand. Grip the wand tightly and make sure the audience cannot see the elastic!

Attach one of the buttons to the elastic and thread the elastic through the tubing. Pull the elastic out through the other end and attach the other button. The elastic should now be quite taut.

Make your 'magic' wand rise on its own by slowly releasing your grip on it. The elastic will go back up inside the tubing. It really is amazing!

# MAGIC TUBES

**This trick will take some time to prepare but it's well worth the effort. You are bound to get plenty of applause!**

### Magic tubes

You are going to make a bottle of mouth-watering fizzy orange appear from nowhere! You'll need a sheet each of blue and red paper and three sheets of black paper measuring 60cm wide and 25cm deep.

Glue the sheet of blue paper to a sheet of black paper. Using the illustration above as a guide, cut a pattern of holes. Bring the short ends together to make a tube and glue them in place.

Make a similar tube from the red and black paper 24cm deep. Overlap the short ends a little bit more to make a slightly narrower tube. Do the same thing with the remaining sheet of black paper, again making the tube slightly shorter and narrower.

Set up the tubes before your audience arrives! Put the black tube on the table with the bottle of orange inside it. Cover it with the red tube and finally the blue tube.

*Make sure the holes face your audience*

When you have your audience's attention, lift off the blue tube and hold it up so that they can see it is black inside. Put your hand through it to show it is empty. Replace it over the red tube.

The audience will not be able to see the black tube. They will think it is the inside of the blue tube!

Look carefully! There is nothing whatsoever inside this tube

Now lift out the red tube and show that it too is empty. Wave your magic wand, say the magic words and pull the bottle out of the black tube!

You can make all sorts of things appear magically but make sure that they will fit in the black tube!

# VANISHING COIN

**Simple to prepare and even easier to perform, this trick will baffle your audience! There is plenty of scope for some good magician's patter.**

### The trick
Tell your audience that you are going to make a coin disappear. Show them the board, the glass without the cover, the cover, and the coin!

Be careful that your audience doesn't see the underside of the glass with its false bottom

Circle of felt or paper to make a false bottom

Use a glass that is not too big and will fit comfortably in your hand

Make sure you can lift the cover on and off easily

With a bit of a flourish put the cover over the glass. Then place the glass with its cover over the coin. Wave your wand over the glass and say some magic words.

### Getting ready
Cover a square of cardboard with some coloured felt or paper. Or, simply lay the felt or paper on a table top. Using the same colour, draw round the rim of a glass and cut out a circle. Glue the circle to the rim of the glass so that it has a false bottom. Make a paper cover to fit round the glass from a different colour of paper.

Lift the cover carefully off the glass and surprise, surprise the coin has vanished completely! Your audience won't believe how easily you have performed this trick. Of course, you know that the coin is really hidden by the false bottom on the glass.

Be careful not to nudge the glass when you put the cover on

You saw it with your very eyes! Where has it gone?

Now you can baffle your audience again by making the coin reappear. Simply do the trick in reverse. Put the cover back on the glass.

Grip the cover and glass firmly so the glass doesn't slip out

Say the magic words and lift both the glass and its cover in one movement. The coin that was hidden appears magically! As with all magic tricks, don't let the audience persuade you to do it again.

# IT'S A SNIP!

**A pair of scissors is the most important prop for these two impressive tricks. You will also need a steady hand and lots of practice!**

### Cut and mend

Hold a length of cord between your thumb and first finger. Take a short length of the same cord and make it into a loop. Hide it as shown. With your other hand take the bottom of the loop and tuck it up under your thumb. At the same time, push the short loop up.

The audience can now see the top of the short loop

Use a pair of scissors to cut through the short loop. The audience will think you have cut through your long length! Trim off all the ends, letting the short loop fall to the floor with the other pieces.

This is the side of your hand that the audience never sees

The audience knows nothing about the secret short loop!

Ask someone in the audience to pull the end of the cord nearest them. Hey presto! It is still in one piece!

## Magic envelope

First prepare your envelope. Cut a small hole out of the back and two slits at either side.

THIS is the side the audience sees!

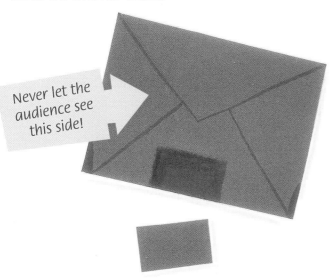

Never let the audience see this side!

Make it look as if you are struggling slightly to cut through the cord!

Thread a length of cord through the slits. You will be able to see it through the small hole! Now the trick is prepared and ready to try out on your audience.

Tell your audience that you are going to cut through the envelope and cord. Before you start, secretly hook out a loop of cord through the hole at the back. Put the blade of the scissors UNDER this loop and cut through the envelope. Invite someone to pull an end of the cord. They will be amazed to find it in one piece!

You can use ribbon but make sure the slits and hole are big enough

Keep the blade of the scissors under the cord

# BODY POWER

**Your body has its own built in magic. You just need to know how to unlock it. Here are a few tricks to astound your friends.**

Tell a friend or someone in your audience that you can make sausages appear in front of their very eyes! Ask them to hold their two first fingers touching in front of their eyes and stare hard at the spot where they join. What happens after a few seconds?

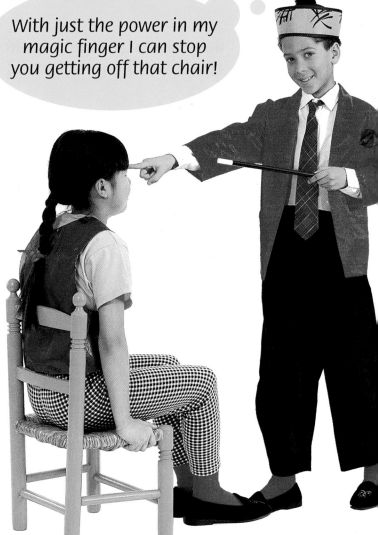

With just the power in my magic finger I can stop you getting off that chair!

Help! I'm seeing flying sausages!

Try moving your fingers apart to make a floating sausage!

### Magic finger

Ask someone to sit all the way back on a straight-backed chair holding the edges of the seat. Stand in front and press your first finger against their forehead. Challenge them to get up. They will be amazed to find that all their strength seems to have gone!

### 1,2,3...oops!

You have the magic power to make someone fall over without even touching them! Tell them to stand with one leg slightly raised and count up to 10. They will be able to do this easily. Now tell them you can make them fall over! Put a blindfold round their eyes and move away. Ask them to raise their leg again and count to 10. By the time they get to 3 or 4 they will be wobbling all over the place!

### Moving pencil

Hold a pencil at arm's length and line it up with something in the distance. Shut each eye in turn. The pencil will jump from side to side!

*Some unknown force is making my pencil move!*

# WANT A BET?

**All magicians have a few card tricks up their sleeve!**
**This one and the one on the next page depend on remembering the 'key' card.**

*Fanning cards out like this is useful for lots of tricks!*

Pick someone out of the audience to be your helper. Give them a big welcome and ask them to shuffle a pack of cards well.

Fan the pack out face down and ask your helper to pick a card and remember it.

*Key card on bottom. Helper's chosen card on top*

*Make sure nobody sees you looking at the key card*

As the helper hands the pack back, sneak a quick glance at the bottom card. Make sure they don't see you looking! The card you have glimpsed is called the 'key' card and it is very important that you remember it until the end of the trick.

Gather the cards into a neat pile making sure that the key card is on the bottom. Tell your helper to put their chosen card back face down on top of the pack.

Cut the pack by taking the top half and placing it face down on the table. Put the remaing cards, also face down, on top.

The key card will now be on top of the chosen card. The helpers chosen card will move to the middle of the pack.

Tell your helper that you are now going to find their chosen card. Start dealing the cards out face up in a line. When you turn over the key card you know that the next one will be the chosen card. Don't say anything just yet! Turn over a few more cards, getting more and more excited.

Now is the time to offer your bet. Tell your helper that you bet that the next card you turn over will be their card. Of course they will think you've got it wrong and will accept the bet eagerly. For the finale, ignore the card in your hand and with a flourish turn over the correct card on the table!

This is one bet I know for sure I'll win!

# SNAP!

**Here is another amazing card trick which depends on using a 'key' card. You will need two packs of cards – one for yourself and one for your chosen helper.**

Tell your helper that you can read his mind and that because of this you will end up choosing EXACTLY the same cards. Explain that they should do exactly what you do.

Shuffle a pack of cards and make sure that your helper does the same. Take a quick, secret look at the bottom card of your pack. This is the all important key card.

Swap packs with your helper. Fan your cards out face down and choose a card. Tell your helper to do the same with his pack and to remember what the card is, keeping it a secret.

*I must remember the key card*

*stare deeply into your helper's eyes*

The only card *you* have to remember is the key card. Both of you should gather your packs together and put your chosen cards on top of each pack. Now you should both cut your packs and swap again.

**24**

Tell your helper to look at his pack and find his chosen card. At the same time you look through your pack to find the key card.
The card to the right of the key card is the one your helper chose.

This is the key card

This is the chosen card

You chose the Queen of Hearts!

Lay it face down on the table and tell your helper to lay his chosen card next to it. When you turn over the two cards they will be exactly the same and there will be amazement all round!

# TIPS

★ When you are taking a quick glimpse at the key card try diverting your audience's attention by talking to them.
★ Practise shuffling, cutting and spreading cards into a fan.

# SECCRET SHELF

**With just a little preparation before your show, you can set up a simple trick that will completely baffle your audience. You could use it for the grand finale!**

Gather together some small objects. Put them in the middle of a square scarf and gather up the edges. Slip an elastic band round the four corners to secure the bundle. Put the bundle on the secret shelf.

Bundle in place on secret shelf

**The shelf**
To make the secret shelf you'll need a small, sturdy cardboard box, such as a shoe box. Cut a section from the box like the one in the picture above.

Put sweets and small toys inside the bundle

Look out for a large cardboard box to make into your magic table for the show. Cover it with a big tablecloth or a length of fabric. Tape, or glue the secret shelf to the back of your magic table. Make sure it is covered by the magic cloth so your audience cannot see it.

No, I'm sorry I can't tell you how to do this trick – it's magic!

Now for the easy part! Dip your hand into the hat and slip the elastic band off the bundle. Produce the scarf and all the other objects one after the other! The audience will be amazed. When they saw the hat a few seconds ago it was empty!

Let the audience see that your hat is completely empty and then place it, brim down, on the table. Now for the clever part! Grip the hat by the brim. As you lift it, take hold of the top of the bundle between your thumb and the brim. Swing it into the hat as it is turned over. This part needs lots of practise so that you can do it in one smooth movement.

# BEFORE THE SHOW!

**Now you are an expert magician. You know how to do lots of different tricks and it's time to try them out in front of a real audience.**

### Let everyone know

Decide on a date for your show, making sure you have plenty of time to organize everything. Send invitations to your friends telling them where and when the show is taking place. Posters are also a good way of spreading the word.

### Planning the programme

Don't make your show last too long! Your audience will get tired and you may start making mistakes. Have a pause for drinks and biscuits half way through. Write a list of the tricks you will be performing. Start with something impressive but not too difficult to get into the swing of things.

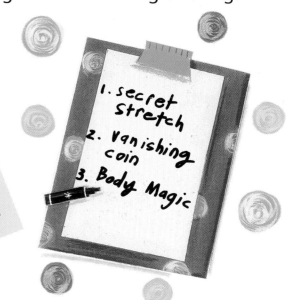

1. Secret Stretch
2. Vanishing coin
3. Body Magic

Make your own posters and invitations using paints, coloured paper and card

### Word perfect

Practise your tricks over and over again! Try performing in front of a mirror and use your best friends and family for a trial run. You could put on a full-scale dress-rehearsal the day before your show.

*I'll be glad when it's time for the show!*

*He looks like a star!*

## Be organized

You will probably need quite a few props for your show. Make sure you have exactly what you need beforehand and that you lay things out so you know where everything is.

A special stage will make your performance look extra professional. Make your own from large sheets of cardboard covered with coloured paper

*What do I have to do?*

A prop box is good for keeping things together

Don't forget the magic hat!

29

# HEY PRESTO

It's time for the show! Make sure you wake up early so you can have a final run through of your tricks. Check to make sure all your props are in the right place.

Ladies and gentlemen, I'd like to introduce you to Marvellous Milton. He'll amaze you with his extraordinary magic powers!

A good introduction will set the scene and get the audience excited

THE MORE YOU PRACTISE, THE BETTER YOUR PERFORMANCE WILL BE!

★

WRITE OUT A LIST OF PROPS SO THAT YOU DON'T FORGET ANYTHING

★

NEVER, EVER GIVE AWAY A MAGIC TRICK

★

DON'T WORRY IF SOMEONE IN THE AUDIENCE THINKS THEY KNOW HOW YOU HAVE DONE A TRICK. MAKE A JOKE OF IT AND CARRY ON

Good magicians need good assistants! Apart from setting up the props beforehand, they can assist throughout the performance by passing props and helping when another pair of hands is needed.

Helpers should also look the part and dress up for the performance

I can see inside your mind! I even know what card you are going to choose. Let me prove it!

If you appear to be confident and in control of things, your audience will be convinced that you really do have magic powers. Starting with a trick that you are particularly good at will help give you the confidence to go on to some of your more difficult ones.

Magic wand to give you special power

Props arranged so you know exactly where everything is

Jacket with pockets inside and outside!

Keep up your 'patter' with the audience. It will help to involve them. Pause when people clap at your amazing skill and never let anyone persuade you to repeat a trick for the second time!

Make your table look special by covering it with a long piece of fabric

'Magic' stage made from cardboard and paper stars

# INDEX

ABRACADABRA!
*I'm about to disappear.*
GOODBYE!